MY WORLD OF POETRY

KASHVEE AGRAWAL

Made with ♥ on the Notion Press Platform
www.notionpress.com

Contents

Preface *v*

Foreword *vii*

Prologue *ix*

About The Author *xi*

Acknowledgements *xiii*

1. Nobody In My World 1
2. Never Quit 2
3. Once Upon A Time In 2020 3
4. Dignity 4
5. Everyone Is Different 5
6. The Happy Pandemic 6
7. ❤ A Special Enchantment ❤ 7
8. They Say 8
9. The Magic Of Nature 9
10. The Stars That Shine For Me 10
11. Believe In Yourself 11
12. Maths For Middle School 12
13. What Is Christmas? 13
14. Never Trust A Mirror 15
15. A World Without Mathematics 16
16. Success 17
17. Ahilyabai Holkar 18
18. A Quarrel With A Loved One 19
19. The Maths Garden 20

Contents

20. As Bright Fills Gloom 21

Preface

This little book, is very special for me and for everyone who have helped me during journey of
this book. True in its very respect, this book is a book for short poetry, created over the last 5
years. This book is also to remind us all that poetry is not just an old- time thing and how
important it is to respect this art of writing words into a beautiful creation. The main
motivation and people who inspired me to write this book are my parents and friends, who
always motivate me and encourage me with topics and ideas to write on. I am also an avid
reader and every book that i read- whether fiction or fantasy; has helped me get new topics
and create new poems. This book is truly a tribute to all those people.

Poetry is a much negotiated career, so many people have demotivated me along the way,
however, there are people who have always inspired & motivated me and in fact turned
these demotivations to be rather helpful. This book came into being to share my love for
poetry with all of you, in hopes that you would like it too. This journey of poetry started around

5 years ago and ever since then, has taught me a lot of new things. Now, here I am, writing my
journey into a book for you all, hoping you enjoy it as much as we do.....

Thank You

Best Wishes

Kashvee Agrawal

Foreword

My World of Poetry- A journey of Inspiration’ is a collection of poems written over the last 5 years, starting at the age of just 7. While I have written hundreds of poems during this period, I have selected some of my beloved key-creations for this book.

This book has poems of different genres and is fit for every mood. There are poems on several topics like motivation, self-experiences, subjects of our school, festivals and people who one should always remember. This book has always been my dream and now it is a dream that I would love to share with all of you. A lot of people think that poetry is an old-time thing. However, I always love to write poems on various topics and in different languages, and with the help of this book, I would want to change this perception and hopefully this work will motivate my fellow writers to follow their passion and to share their art with everyone.

Well I truly hope you enjoy reading this book as much as I enjoyed making it!!

Thank You

Regards

Kashvee Agrawal (Author)

Prologue

"Believe you can you are halfway there!"

About The Author

Kashvee Agrawal

The author of this book, Kashvee Agrawal was born in Jaipur, Rajasthan on 13th June 2010 to
Dr.Monika and Sachin Agrawal. After living the first few months of her life in Jaipur, at her
paternal home, she moved to Gurugram, Haryana after her father's transfer. After
studying in a preschool during her kindergarten years, she was admitted to a formal school in
Gurugram DLF Phase-III in April 2015 in first grade. At the age of

6, she started writing her first story book 'Fascinating Tales by Kashvee'which is a collection of short stories, and kept writing short stories. She wrote her first poem at the age of 6, on the topic of 'Summer'. Ever since then, she kept going and has now written many poems and a few stories. She has written many poems on many topics and subjects, for many occasions and school competitions. She presently studies in the same school in grade 8th and has been recognized as the Middle Prefect.

She has amazing friends and parents who always support her and encourage her. She will keep writing poems and will continue to publish books for you all to read.....This is her first book so Thank you for supporting her.....We hope you like it..!

Acknowledgements

I(Kashvee) would love to thank my parents- Dr.Monika and SachinAgrawal for always encouraging me and helping me for the best. I would also thank my friends and my teachers for always helping me and encouraging me. I would love to thank my little brother Kaveesh for being a major part of my bliss. I would also like to thank god for always helping me from above...

THANK YOU..!

Acknowledgments

[illegible]

1. Nobody in my world

1) Nobody in my world

Nobody in my world is perfect,
Nobody is born with defect.
Too fat, too thin, too tall too short,
It's all just a game,
For this game, young souls wouldn't shatter themselves just to own
fame.
Nobody in my world would strive for affection,
If everyone lived my world, there'll only be love, no perfection.
It's all that in your heart,?
It's all that in your beneath.
It's all that you can dart,
Trust, faith, love and belief.

2. Never Quit

2) Never Quit

When things go so wrong, as they will,
Don't be sad and stay strong.
When the road you are on seems uphill,
Don't go astray and keep still.
When the fund is low and debts are high,
Keep on a smile, and don't sigh.
When life presses you, bit by bit,
Stay as you are, work hard and don't quit.
Life is a path full of twists and turns,
You will know, gradually as you learn.
When success is far and failure comes your way,
Don't be anxious and always remember, for forever, nothing stays..
Success is just failure, inside out,
It may feel good, no doubt.
You never know the distance, how close you are,
It may be near, when seems far.
So stick to the field till your best hit,
Give your best, things may change, so never quit......

3. Once upon a time in 2020

"*3)Once upon a time in 2020*

With light to the trouble we suffered during those days,
There are just a few things I would like to say.
Alone, a day might feel like an year,
Together, we can even fill this time with cheer.
Alone, we might think we can't defeat you,
Together, as a world, we will beat you.

It all started, once upon a time in 2020,
When the world was changing, and schools got empty.
The world once happy, now became sad,
It was a start to suffer and something bad.
Everyone stayed home, just in case,
and washed our hands more, to be safe.
Sometimes we laughed, sometimes we cried,
It was different for us, staying inside.
Now that we know, rules are boons,
We will keep fighting and end this soon."

4. Dignity

4)Dignity

You get dignity, when you stop thinking wrong,
You get dignity, when your dear ones are along.
You get dignity, when you are in the light,
You get Dignity, when you think you are right
Dignity, is when you take a stand for you,
Without closing your mind for a word of others or two.
Dignity, is being an example of what you want.
Dignity, is avoiding gossip about others or thoughts.
Dignity, is not about what we see,
Its what we do and how we be.
Dignity will be there, if you have good thoughts in your heart.
It will be there for you if you keep doing your part.

5. Everyone is different

"5)Everyone is different

Everybody in this world are not always the same,

For that, whom should we blame.

Well, we have the same eyes and nose and same ears

But different concepts and types of what one wears.

Some are kind, but some are cruel,

Some are rich, but some are poor.

Everybody isn't same after all,

Some are big, some are small,

Some are short, while some are tall.

Some have a good time, Some have a bad

But live together at one place,

different difficulties each have to face.

After all life isn't easy

And that is the similarity between us all."

6. The Happy Pandemic

“6) The Happy Pandemic

YOUR SMILE MAKES ME LAUGH,
YOUR SMILE PASSES MY DAY.
YOUR SMILE GIVES ME HAPPINESS,
IN EVERY SINGLE WAY.

YOUR SMILE‘S LIKE FLU,
IT CAN BE CONTAGIOUS.
YOU SMILED AT ME TODAY,
EVER SINCE, I HAVE BEEN SMILING TOO.

I FIND YOUR SMILE TO BE OF WORTH,
YOUR SMILE, IT CAN CHANGE THE EARTH .
I AM SURE NOW THAT IT IS INFECTIOUS,
AND WE CAN GET INFECTED.
LET’S START A PANDEMIC,
AND GET THE WORLD "SMILE DETECTED".

❤”

7. ❤ A SPECIAL ENCHANTMENT ❤

"7)❤ A SPECIAL ENCHANTMENT ❤

How can one doubt it,

When rainbows shimmer and flowers bloom.

The rays of the sun shining towards the morning dew,

Reflecting MAGIC, somewhere plenty, somewhere few.

The rise of dawn and shine of the Moon,

Telling us, Life is a boon.

A boon made from magic,

A boon made from truth.

Telling us, magic lies in its roots.

Magic lies in everything, You just need a peek,

To a magnificent world, where nobody is weak.

The freshness in orchards, Softness in grass,

All from magic, through a wand or looking glass.

All this gives us just a hint about this SPECIAL ENCHANTMENT.

The majestic sight developed through magic....."

8. They Say

"8) They say......... ♥

It's this thing that every other person says when we meet,

They say I can't be a poet, for there'll be failures to beat.

They say if I became a poet, I wouldn't be able to survive,

I say, if I follow my passion, I shall surely survive.

They say poetry is a hobby, it can't be my career,

If you ask me, with just my words, I can push any barrier.

To all those other people, who think like I do,

Keep it up and do what you like to........."

9. The Magic Of Nature

9)The Magic Of Nature

To the leaves that rustle and the river that flows,
Seldom let the nature go numb.
To the bark that stands and the plant that grows,
The sound of nature never be mum.
To the stones that fall, and the birds that chirp,
Seldom let the breeze come still.
To the whistling wing and dropping hail,
Seldom let the magic of nature fail.
It's the plight of nature to bear us man,
To demolish thy beauty and immense sanity,
What's there for nature to bring back, if it can,
For man tampers nature to celebrate inhumanity...

10. The Stars that shine for me

“*10) The Stars that shine for me*

They say, look up at the stars,
So bright yet far away.
Although , I know by morning they will be gone,
Still I wish they would stay.
I'd stare them all night,
To see how they shine.
They shine all through the dark, making it feel bright.
For some say, our future lies beneath them,
Written in their shine.
On that dark, empty space,
I take a lookout at all the stars, to see which one has mine.
I ask them, what will be? But they are too far away,
Even if they would answer my quests I would not here a word they
say.
But i will wait and watch every night,
For endless spans of time. Until I learn what they say,
And all the secrets will be mine.....
”

11. Believe In Yourself

11)Believe In Yourself

Believe in yourself, and in your dream,
Keep Dreaming, impossible it may seem.
Somewhere, someday, you shall be there,
Success might feel far, but really its near.
Mountains shall fall and seas shall divide,
Before the one, the one who is the stride.
Always remember to take the long path,
day-by-day,
Keep the hard-work high, pushing all obstacles
away.
Believe in you, and in your plan,
Don't say you cannot, but say you can.
These prizes of life we fail to win,
All because we doubt the power within....

12. Maths for Middle School

"12) Maths for Middle School

Math, math, it's a subject at school,
Math, math, it's really cool.
That's what we think, until we enter middle school.
Math, math, it becomes a bakery and sells pi(?),
Math, math, you can't be shy.
Math, math, everything has an angle,
Math, math, The numbers make you tangle.
Math, math, same after hours,
It's all about length, width and how far.
?— change to congruence and area,
Math, math, can give you a math-malaria.
Math, math, better make it happy then bad,
Oh its math, you can't be sad?
After all, math makes us what we are,
Math is bliss, that needs to be spread far.
So let's study hard and see what can be done,
to spread the happiness and make math the one........"

13. What is Christmas?

"13) What is Christmas?

What is Christmas, I ask myself?
Is it just the gifts or the cookies on the shelf?
Is it just the tree or the lights?
Is it just an old man flying up high.
There's more to christmas
Than lights and cheer
It's the spirit of giving and joy,
Which lasts for all the year.
It's love, and it's honour to Jesus.
It's hope in hearts again.
For peace and goodwill,
And wellbeing of all our men.
Its love, its merry, its honour,
Its Christmas in every corner.
Is mine, it is yours, it is ours,
Its hope and love spreading far.
Its joy and cheer, here and there,
Cuz', its Christmas-Christmas everywhere.
It's for our people,
Our family and friends

Let the cheer spread

And let this spirit never end..

”

14. Never Trust a Mirror

14) Never Trust a Mirror

Never trust a mirror, for it always lies,
Apart its evident deliberation, the rest lies in surmise.
A mirror seldom captures my smile, the one I smile for truth,
A mirror is the one, causing tears in the youth.
Never trust a mirror, for its evident for ones skin,
For it never declares worth, of your powers within.
Never trust a mirror, for it doesn't show the world through what you see,
It's seldom caught praising, for the person you can be,
Never trust a mirror, for no prophet durst declare your price,
Never trust a mirror, for it always lies....

15. A World Without Mathematics

"15)A World Without Mathematics

Imagine a World,

Without Mathematics,

No rulers, No scales,

No inches, No feats,

No dates or Numbers,

On houses or streets.

No prices, No weights,

No determining Heights.

No hours running through,

Either days or nights.

No zeroes, No birthdays,

No ways to subtract,

All those hours of Guesswork,

Surrounding the fact,

But how is this world possible, in spite of that,

GOD USED MATHEMATICS TO CREATE THIS PRICELESS

WORLD....!

"

16. Success

16) Success

Success is not a number, a thing or
someplace real,
It's all about the attitude and dreams of
what you feel.
Success is a nothing, a nuisance after all.
If your happiness and bliss is gone,
What's in making billions,
If its yield is at a hefty cost.
History might judge us, but what matters
is us now,
Enjoying everything we do, it is hard to
do somehow?
You may go in pursuit of success,
It is in the reach of your hand you know,
Just enjoy the things around you and
smile,
And watch your success grow..

17. Ahilyabai Holkar

"*17) Ahilyabai Holkar*

Great is my India, where Ahilyabai was born.
Never heard of a woman so great,
Even though, married at the age of 8.
Was a very inspiring soul, a role model for all.
Either at the adult age of 21, or as a 8 year old girl, a girl so small.
A perfect blend of spirituality and leadership,
A great respect towards her Shiv ji and apprenticeship.
Sati, Sutee and Sahamagna.
She did lots for women empowerment.
Oh! How she was just so inspirational,
Ahilyabai Khanderao Holkar, she really was sensational."

18. A Quarrel with a loved one

"18) ♡ A Quarrel with my loved one ♡
I fought with my brother,
Pretending as we couldn't stand each other.
I still don't remember what about,
Hmm, Yes I still have a doubt.
I started to cry bad,
He was startled, thinking i was mad.
As he saw me cry,
he walked sadly to his room nearby.
He started to calm down,
Still, I was up with an angry frown.
After a long time, like 100 years had past,
This quarrel ended at last.
He had come to apologize, saying this cannot always last,
And we really wanted it to solve fast
Now, I thought he was right ,
As he volunteered to end this fight.
At last, we are the best of friends,"

19. The Maths Garden

19)The Maths Garden
Welcome to the maths garden,
where trees bore numbers.
With the faithful teachers, named rolefully
Addition, Subtraction, Measurement,
Multiplaction, Division and much more.
Magic butterflies twirl up and down ,
with answers on their backs.
The kids march with the band,
singing the maths song, won't you sing along.
+, -, *, / are the charms of fairies,
with pencils and papers in their palms.
As a great man has said'' God had also used mathematics
in creating the priceless world''

20. As Bright Fills Gloom

"20) As Bright Fills Gloom

All is calm, All is failing,
As the seas stay still with nothing sailing.
As brightness ascends and shadows arrive,
As the clouds of fog silently creep, the brains strives.
They say joy finds way, though silence creeps.
The joy fades as darkness seeps.
As unspoken words scream in silence,
As questions arise, to resort to violence.
Thoughts wanting to be heard, Wanting to be known,
As limits of depression seem to have outgrown.
Falling into dungeons deep, where darkness resides,
Where there once were boats, now lie tides.
Lights will brighten, faces will alight,
Shadows will fade, ending the prolonged fight.
It's still not night, for bells still ring,
It's still not end for birds still sing.
It's still not day for night still lies,
It's still not free, for chains still severe all ties.
These chains, we will break,
The menace, we will confide,

This phase, we will overcome,

And life would revive.....

- Written and Compiled by KASHVEE AGRAWAL ”

9 798889 862291

Printed by Libri Plureos GmbH in Hamburg,
Germany